Tiger's Adventures *in the* Everglades

VOLUME TWO

As told by T. F. Gato

jay gee heath

Copyright © 2018
All rights reserved. No part of this book may be reproduced, scanned, or transmitted in any form or by any means, electronic or mechanical, including photocopying, recording, or by any information storage and retrieval system, without permission from the copyright owner.

All characters appearing in this work are fictitious. Any resemblance to real persons, living or dead, is purely coincidental. Names, characters, places, and incidents either are the product of the author's imagination or are used fictitiously, and any resemblance to any actual persons, living or dead, events, or locales is entirely coincidental.

ISBN: eBook 978-0-9992454-3-9
ISBN Print Book 978-0-9992454-2-2

Library of Congress Control Number: 2017912570

Publisher
Joyce G Heath, Naples, Fl

ALSO BY JAY GEE HEATH

Right Talents
Right Skills
Right Dreams
Right Response
Right Target
Tiger's Adventures in the Everglades

DEDICATION

To Sam

ACKNOWLEDGEMENT

Thank you for your help and encouragement

Janet Benjamins
Jo Anne Sullivan
Jean Smith

Art by K. T. Gato

As we can all see from the pictures, Tiger is not a Maine Coon cat.

Tiger

TABLE OF CONTENTS

Don't Climb the Coconut 1

Scorpion 17

Killer 37

Killer Sequel 51

Beggar Lice 65

Bacon Wrapped Fried Chicken Nuggets. 83

LIST OF ILLUSTRATIONS

1. Tiger
2. Land Crab
3. Tiger in Coconut
4. Scorpion
5. Tiger Looking at Scorpion
6. Tiger in Surprise
7. Killer
8. Killer and Tiger
9. Two Dogs
10. Hidden Bird
11. Sparrow Hawk
12. Tiger Caught with Nuggets
13. Tiger Climbing Screen

DON'T CLIMB THE COCONUT

It's warm and sunny. A perfect afternoon. Lazy afternoon. I'm half dozing, settled comfortably in the crook of two low branches in a small sea grape with my feet hanging down. It's cool and pleasant here and large round shade leaves rattle and fan me when the wind blows. The tree is called a sea grape because it has clusters of grapes just like real grapes that you find on grape vines or in the grocery store; at least, that's what Boston says. The clumps do look like the bunches she brings home after shopping.

But these grapes are hard dark purple balls. The skin covers a thin layer of fruit wrapped around a large seed. I haven't tried them. Why would I? I've never seen any humans eat them, though Boston and Kevlar made sea grape jelly. Once.

They make prickly pear cactus jelly, too. Boston says the cacti grow well in the Everglades in the dry sandy soil.

Go figure. The pears have sharp prickly spines all over and the first time they made jelly, they said ouch a lot. The next time, they wore thick gloves and used grill tongs to pick up the red fruit and peel off the skin and spines. Boston says some folks cook the fruit with the skin and spines attached and then she shudders. They plonk the pears in water, boil them, mash them, add sugar, pectin, and key lime juice, and end up with jelly.

They make key lime jelly too. I don't know why. But they seem to have fun. I don't bother to watch because they don't use any food I want.

The squirrels eat the grapes. Not the little gray squirrels we had up north. These squirrels are BIG. And they have two big names, the Mangrove Fox squirrel or Big Cypress Fox squirrel. They don't walk like the squirrels up north either, but kind of lumber. Like a 'gator. They are a dark red-brown color and their heads, ears, and nose are black. Look like criminals wearing ski masks. I've never seen them steal anything, but they like the sea grapes.

You'd expect the Mangrove squirrel to be in the mangroves, but he hangs out in the gumbo limbo. The mangroves are strange trees which line the shore and don't mind salt water. I'm real careful around water. Not scared. Just distrustful. Water is sneaky. I like to know where the water is. It tried to drown me not too long ago. Kevlar fished me out as I was going down for the last time. I could have lost one of my nine lives.

There are three kinds of mangroves. The red mangroves have lots of branches, some of which grow down into the water like legs, instead of up into the air. The black mangrove grows by the shore, too, but it pushes short roots straight up through the soil and water to reach the air. The white mangrove grows a little more inland, not in the water. The leaves are all green, not white, or black, or red.

The mangroves have strange proper names, Boston told me. The only one I remember is that the red is a mangle. As if that makes any sense. The sea grapes' scientific name is coccoloba. Not to be confused with the coconut palm or the cocoa tree with the cocoa bean which makes chocolate, something Boston loves. Sometimes names are too confusing. Boston's always discussing flora and fauna. Two words that I mix up. I can't remember which is which, I think fauna is animal because Bambi was a fawn and flora is a plant like a flower. I don't remember everything she tells me.

Boston likes words and knows all kinds of stuff. Not just the word meanings, but also their origins and uses. The guys found out and, at first, teased her. Then challenged her. They'd throw a word at her and if she could explain where it came from and what it meant, they'd buy the beer. If she failed, she'd buy. They did that instead of arm wrestling.

The men laugh, fairly sure of themselves, but they always lose the contest. So far, she hasn't had to buy any drinks. They keep trying, digging up new words they don't understand, but she can always explain the origin and meaning. They check her answers with the dictionary.

Well, I was dozing in the sea grape until this flock of red-winged blackbirds flew in. Red-winged because they have a red, orange, yellow patch on their shoulders. The males do. The females are just plain brown. The birds are always chattering, chirp, chiro, chirp, up-a-treeeee, up-a-treeeee, up-a-treeeee. That's what woke me, the noise. I don't think they listen to each other, just chirp. Attracted by the grapes they hop about the branches. Always on the move, always chattering.

So much for my nap. I'm a cat, so dozing and lazing are my nature.

I climb down and look around for another spot to sleep, but everything looks the same as it did before my nap. The same as when I came out. The same as yesterday and last week. This group of sea grape trees. The gumbo limbo across the way. It has a dark red bark that peels and feels funny, so I don't climb it even though it has nice thick low branches. Besides the squirrel is up there, hanging out.

Right now, he's ignoring me. He does that a lot. You'd think he would be afraid of me, after all I'm a Maine Coon cat. These birds should be scared too, but they act like I'm not even here. Humpf.

I'm not going to the shoreline and eye the three coconut palm trees standing at the edge of the paved area, their green fronds pointing every which way guarding bunches of coconuts. Large brown almost ripe coconuts, large green ones, and small green ones the size of tennis balls.

Two trees straight and tall. One slanted and sloping. Hmm. I've never climbed a coconut. Well, I did start up one of the tall ones once. I only got a short way when I realized I wasn't going to make it to the top. I'm a Maine Coon cat so I have a bit of weight, and I'm not so used to climbing. Weight wasn't my only problem. A blue hard-shelled thing was looking me in the eye, his pincers opening and closing like a crab. Clacking. This was a tough lookin' hombre. Big. Bigger than the little crabs that run all over the mangrove roots and along the shoreline. His body was almost as big as my head, and kind of boxy and rounded, about the size of a nice juicy hamburger with bun. He had his claws open pointing at me in a boxer stance. His eyes stood on top of waving stalks, bugging out on the top of his head. I lost my grip and slid four inches.

Land Crab

"Land crab," Boston, my lady, explained, plucking me off the tree and setting me on the ground. Rescuing me.

Wasn't any way I would get around the clacking crab, so I let her.

Do land crabs eat cats?

And what was the stupid land crab doing in a tree?

I understand blue crabs. They are a deep dark blue and flat, shaped like a sliced bread ham sandwich. They live in the salt water. Boston and Kevlar catch them with fishing poles baited with chicken necks. They boil and shell the crabs. Seems like a lot of work, when you could just eat the chicken necks. But blue crab meat is pretty good.

Boston and Kevlar have never tried to catch land crabs. Boston says they're terrestrial, they live on land, on the ground, not in the water. And not in trees. They dig deep burrows and eat fruit and berries, leaves, and small insects. That's what Boston read to me that night. She likes to learn and says if she repeats stuff out loud to me she remembers it; but she never said anything about land crabs climbing a tree. Or if they eat cats.

Hamburgers, ham sandwiches. I'm sort of hungry. I look toward the house, but it's not meal time yet. I tilt my head. Still considering the coconut trees. Hmm. Not the tall straight ones. I study the short, slanted coconut. Piece of cake. I glance over at Boston, my lady. She is here too, sitting in the shade painting a canvas. I bring her with me when I come out.

I meander over. The squirrel is watching. I don't even

need to climb this sloping coconut and I walk up the trunk. It's like a steep hill. But the last three feet are straight up. I can climb three feet. I scurry up. It's hard but only a short distance, and when I reach the top I scoot around a hanging frond and under another and climb up onto a bunch of brown coconuts. And scamper over another frond which puts me beside a cluster of green coconuts. I start to climb out on top of one, but it's slippery and I can't get a grip, so I edge back and search for another path. I can see a stair-step route up and around and I continue on. Frond, coconut, frond, frond, coconut. It's dicey, but soon I'm as high as I can go. I'm above all the coconuts and the fronds are all pointing straight up. I'm not stupid. I can see they won't hold my weight. This spot is where I saw that raccoon last week, and I can smell him a little. My perch is shaky and wobbly and sways with the breeze, not a very secure spot and now that I think about it, the raccoon didn't look too comfortable.

Hmm. The view is not all that much different up here in the coconut than the one I have on the front porch on the second floor. I look down on the sea grapes and the noisy birds, way above the spot where I just took my nap. I'm about equal to the middle of the gumbo limbo where the squirrel is still watching me. I can see over to the patio where the mocking bird is picking hot red peppers off Kevlar's potted plant and eating them whole. Popping them, well like sunflower seeds. The mocker must have an iron stomach and no taste buds in his beak. The peppers are so hot they make my eyes water if I get too near.

I see the round table where the folks meet after work and the trailers which are parked in front of the far tree line across the street. The mangrove shoreline in the other direction.

Boring. And uncomfortable. And it quickly gets old. I'm suddenly thirsty and hungry and turn to head down. And slip. Scrabble for a purchase. (Scrabble and purchase? Aren't those funny words.) I get a secure grip. I don't see the opening I climbed through to get up here. I head back down very carefully and slowly clamber and crawl all around the top, a full circle back to where I started. I think. Boston would say, circumnavigate, walk around. Walked the full circumference. Circumference is like a circle. Not circumvent because that would be dodge around or avoid.

Why am I thinking about words?

Because I might be stuck. And if I'm stuck, I may need Boston.

I complete another circuit and find a place to try.

Start down. Head first, like the squirrels.

I get one step and realize this isn't going to work.

The fronds sway like, well, like they're being rocked by waves. I tilt my head and try to remember how I climbed down from the sea grape.

Didn't. Jumped. That's when I remember, cats back down trees. I scramble to turn, but now I can't see the path. I edge down blindly and bump into coconuts. Twist a little and bump into fronds.

Try a few more times.

Try a different spot. Same results.

I try head first again. But now that I remember it's wrong, I can't hold myself and tumble down a level. Oops.

I try backwards again and bump into more stuff. Can't find the path. Now I am concerned and take a rest on a coconut. I'm really tired of being up here. And hungry. The squirrel is still watching. I think he may be laughing. Time to call for help.

"Merowww."

Boston is still out here, but I can't see her.

"Meroooww." A little louder. She wouldn't leave without me.

"Tiger? Where are you?"

"Meroww."

Both she and Kevlar walk out from the garage shading their eyes with their hands, staring up into the tree. I try a soft meow.

It's Kevlar who spots me, points me out. "Up there in the little coconut."

Little?

"Between the palm fronds. See? How did he get up there?"

Well, duh. Climbed?

"Meow?"

I show them I can't get down. Edge forward. Back up. Repeat.

Tiger in Coconut

"Can't you get down?" Kevlar asks.

"Meow." I edge forward and back again. I don't make a snide remark this time; after all, I want their help. Then I fake an attempt to jump.

"Don't jump. Don't jump," Boston pleads and I stumble backward, almost losing my grip, but I dig in.

"You have to get him down," she wails to Kevlar.

Yes.

"The cat got up there; the cat can get down," he says. He's not really a cat person. Not yet. He joined our family after we moved down here to the Everglades. That night when Boston drove us to the end of the road and turned left... and then drove to the end of the road. He was already living here. I'm teaching him the important status of cat, but he's a work in progress.

I think I hear laughter in his voice.

He better not be laughing.

"No. He's stuck. You have to rescue him." She's begging now. Good for her. I give him a stare. My poor, pitiful cat stare. Not that I am poor or pitiful, but I am stuck. I look at him hopefully.

His lips twitch.

He better not laugh.

He sort of scowls, shakes his head. "Stupid cat," he mutters under his breath.

I hear him. He'll pay later.

He measures distances with his eyes. "I think, if I back my truck up, I can reach him from the roof."

Boston pleads. "Yes. Yes. Please. Do it. He's stuck. Hurry."

Yes. Do it. Don't stand there talking about it, get me down.

He walks to his truck, gets in and backs it slowly until the bed is under the tree, the cab a little forward of my position. He gets out. "You think he's going to let me grab him?"

"Probably." She shrugs her shoulders hopefully.

He mutters under his breath again; I can't make out the words, and he jumps in the bed of the truck and climbs up on the cab.

And we're looking each other in the eye.

"You better not claw me," he warns.

Like I would hurt my rescuer. I edge out a tad to demonstrate my good intentions and he reaches for me.

At that moment, Ranger Bob and Wolf his cat come out of their apartment and stop on the stoop to stare. Wolf and I have that détente thing going since Bob and Boston said they would ground us, make us stay indoors, if we fight. I don't attack him; he doesn't beat me up. But he still sneers at me.

Bob laughs. Wolf snickers.

Bob hollers over. "Tiger's stuck in the tree? Can't get down? Want some help." He laughs harder. At me. And that crazy Wolf is watching wide eyed.

Not bad enough Wolf can whomp me, now he's laughing at me. Sniggering. Bet he's making up jingles. *Kitty, kitty, stuck in a tree. Misses his supper, tee hee hee.* I can just hear him. He'll be mocking me when I get down.

I back up a tad. Maybe I don't want to be rescued. Not while they're watching. Not 'til they leave.

But Bob sits on a step, lifts his coffee cup, and takes a sip, settling in. "Maybe you should leave him up there until he figures it out. If he figures it out."

Wolf snickers again. *Like he has never been stuck in a tree?*

I edge back a tad more and notice the squirrel is laughing, too. More at the whole situation, I think. Not at me.

"Seriously, though, you want some help?" Bob asks.

"Nah," Kevlar says. "He's not stuck. We are in the midst of a power struggle and he's in trouble."

What? What power struggle?

"This animal has to learn who is boss, and I'm going to teach him. I told him to stay out of the coconut trees and I look out the window to see Mr. Smarty Pants playing king of the mountain in the top of the coconut."

Smarty Pants?

Kevlar is still complaining to Bob. "Tiger doesn't want to get down. Once I get him out of there I'm placing him under house arrest for a week."

I cringe. House arrest?

Wait. He never told me that. He never told me not to climb the coconut.

He whispers, "Work with me here, Tiger. Maybe we can both come out of this with some pride and our reputations intact. We can con them. Make them think, I'm dragging you out of the tree to punish you, not rescuing you."

Then, more loudly, he says, "Don't you move, Tiger. You're in enough trouble already. Don't you disobey me. I'm taking you out of this tree and locking you in the bathroom."

He winks.

Hah?

He says, in an undertone, "Of course I'm not locking you in the bathroom. You'd scatter the litter all over and shred the toilet paper. Probably chew on the toothpaste tube and lick my toothbrush."

Yeah, I would. Well, all except licking his toothbrush, I hadn't thought of that but it seems like a good idea.

I wonder how he'd know if I licked it. I guess I could leave teeth marks on the handle.

I snarl once for show, a timid snarl, and he winks again and reaches up and grabs me by my shoulders and lifts me off my perch.

I growl and we continue the charade. I hope it's a charade. He wraps me tight in one arm, jumps back down into the bed of the truck, and then out. He sets me on my feet. "Bad cat," he says in a stern voice. "I told you to stay out of that tree."

I turn my back on him. Flick my tail. Lick my front paw. And grab a sneaky peek at Wolf. Not laughing at me anymore. Looks impressed.

Wow.

Boston is struggling to hold in a giggle. "Bad cat. Go upstairs and get in the house."

I sneer at her, but she snatches me up.

"Don't you ignore me." She stomps upstairs and inside with Kevlar following right behind.

As soon as the door is closed, they fall on each other laughing.

"You are such a wonderful cat person," she tells him.

"Think we fooled them?" Kevlar asks. "We can't have them believing Tiger couldn't climb down a coconut tree."

"Ah ha," she says between giggles. "You should have seen Bob's face. And Wolf looked awestruck. Tiger may be his new role model."

I prance over to sit in front of the refrigerator.

I'll eat first, then nap. All in all, it's been a good day.

And I'm going to have to think about that toothbrush. Wouldn't be any fun to lick it if Kevlar didn't know. Couldn't do it in front of him. Guess I could lick it and chew the handle and knock it off the counter. Or carry it to my litter box. Hmm

Not today though. I owe him.
But I still deserve a reward.
Yawn.

SCORPION

That's an odd shaped leaf. About two inches long.
Not a leaf. Maybe a small lizard or a fishing lure, like the ones Kevlar sometimes uses.

Just lying there.

I walk over to check it out. Might be fun.

I approach cautiously. This is the wilderness and there are some ugly things out here. A cat, even a Maine Coon cat like me has to be watchful. I reach out to tap it carefully with my paw. Carefully, because, I've learned the hard way not to sniff things first, at least, not until I know it's safe

Yipe. I freeze.

It's alive. I perk up my ears.

It twists and raises its tail over its head. Points the ugly thing at me. And strikes.

Instinctively I leap into the air.

I'm too slow. It sticks me with the point of its tail!

That stupid thing.

Ow. It hurts. Even before I land, my paw is burning.

With fire. I land on my injured foot, but it doesn't hold my weight and I fall hard.

Ow. It hurts. Burns.

I try to shake the burning off, but that only spreads the fiery pain. It hurts worse than anything I've ever felt.

Run. Run. Get away. Ow. Ow. Get away from the fire. I stand and take a step… and am snatched by my lady as I start my sprint. She whips me into the air and under her arm, one hand gripping my paw.

She'd yelled. "No. Tiger. Don't touch that, Tiger." I'd heard her just as I reached out to poke the leaf thing. But I was intent on the leaf and her words didn't register.

Or maybe they did. Sometimes I don't always do what she says. What kind of a cat would I be if I always obeyed her? Besides, I was curious. And I didn't touch the stupid thing. It stung me before I had a chance.

Ow. Ow. Oh. Ow. It hurts.

She grips my leg between her fingers and now it hurt in two places and I need to *RUN*.

But she holds me captured securely in her arms. "Hold still. Moving will spread the poison."

Poison? He stuck me. With poison? Like a snake?

Ow.

I squirm, try to dig in and push off with my back paws, but she holds me tighter, squeezing me to her body with her elbow. I can't get leverage.

Run. Run. Get away. I squirm frantically.

Ow.

"Stop. Just stop," she orders, her voice both stern and soothing.

"Hold still," she says again.

I can't. *Have to run. Get away.*

She carries me up the stairs and into the kitchen. "It's okay," she says, speaking calmly.

It's not okay. My paw hurts. It's burning. It's scorched. It hurts.

She shoves my paw under the faucet and the cold water shocks when it hits me.

No. Not water. I hate water. It's cold.

I try to snatch my paw back, but she's ready for me and doesn't let go; she holds it firmly under the running water.

Is my foot on fire? Is that why it's burning so badly? He set me on fire? Is it scorched? Singed? Is she putting a fire out? I don't smell smoke or burning fur. You never want to smell burning fur.

I look. No smoke. No fire. Just my paw. Wet.

It still burns. The cold water doesn't help.

Run.

I try to twist out of her grasp again. Struggle.

She holds me firmly. Holds my paw under the water. Flushing the burning area.

The water doesn't help. My paw still stings. Like fire. Blistering. Scalding. Searing.

Let me go. Let me go. I can outrace it. Ow.

"Stop. Hold still another minute." She reaches into the cabinet and pulls out something that looks like a salt shaker.

"Meat tenderizer," she says in a calm tone. "It will help. Honest."

No. No. Ow.

My heart is thumping, pounding and I'm out of breath as if I have been running.

Yes. Run. I need to run.

She shakes some white stuff on my paw and rubs it all over. Funny stuff, sort of like salt, but the crystals are long and feathery. It doesn't smell. She makes a paste of it on my paw, talking all the while in her soft, everything is okay tone. "It's okay. It will be better in a minute. Hold still. This will help. Give it a minute."

No. It's not helping! I pant and wail.

"Mrow"

But she talks and rubs. "It will take away the burning. I promise. Hold still. Be patient."

Ow. Oh. Ow. Run.

She isn't listening. "Meat tenderizer. People use it on steaks to make them less chewy.

Who cares. Ow. "Hissss."

"It draws out the poison in insect bites and stings. I don't remember it's proper name, what it's called. Um. Papain, I think."

Pain? Really? She putting more pain on my paw? Ow. Stop it. Stop the fire. Don't put on more.

"This will help with the sting. I promise. Give it a minute."

No. No. let me go.

She's still explaining about the pa pa pain.

"It's an old wives' tale. Using meat tenderizer on stings. But it will work, even if neither of us is an old wife."

Owwww. She's making jokes? While my foot is melting?

She rubs more stuff on and spreads it all through my fur. But it isn't helping. It isn't helping.

"I use it on red ant bites, horse fly and deer fly bites."

It hurts.

She loosens her grip on my paw a second to get more salt, and I shake my foot sending white flakes around the kitchen.

Let me go. Let me go. Running will help.

It's burning so bad. I know I can out-run it, if she'll only let me go.

I squirm, twist.

She rubs more pain stuff onto my paw, replacing what I shook off.

Owww... Let me ......

Hunh?

What?

It doesn't hurt.

My paw doesn't hurt. It stopped burning. It doesn't hurt.

Wow.

But then I worry. Did she cut my paw off?

I'm afraid to look, but I have to see. I peek around.

Oh. Thank goodness. It's still there. All wet and white. And it doesn't hurt. I wiggle my toes, just to double check.

"Hold still," she orders. "You can't shake the paste off. You have to let it do its job. Now hold still."

It doesn't hurt. I relax a little. She feels the change and loosens her grip a tad.

"Okay. I'm going to wash it off."

No. No. don't wash it off. It helps.

I try to pull my paw back, but she renews her grip and I can't pull it away.

She rinses it and shakes on more pain stuff.

"This is called a poultice," she says. Still teaching. Always teaching. I can get a breath now.

Okay. Pole ice? I watch closely as she rubs it in.

She carries me to the bathroom. "We need a non-stick gauze pad, elastic wrap, and maybe a small piece of tape to stick the bandage to your leg. Otherwise you'll shake it off and scatter meat tenderizer all over the house."

I would never do that. I watch her gently wrap my foot. The gauze pad, elastic wrap. The wrap stretches a little and sticks to itself holding the pad in place.

"I have to put on some tape to stick the bandage to your leg. But it will peel off easily."

My paw doesn't burn any longer. It's a relief.

She carries me to the rocking chair where she cuddles me safe in her arms, and rocks whispering to me. My heart slows down, returns to normal. My eyelids are tired.

"See," she says, "water isn't all bad. Sometimes it's good. It can wash a wound. Some people use rubbing alcohol for stings, but I've never tried that because the meat tenderizer has always worked."

I guess, sure. Whatever. I look at my paw in its strange little mitten. Cautiously, I flex my toes inside the bandage. They still work.

"That was a scorpion," she says.

Stupid thing. Rotten, vicious thing stung me.

I hate those things. Hate them. Mean, rotten creatures.
Hate them. Nasty, vicious brutes
They're disgusting.
They don't care who they hurt. Just stick that tail in the air and stab you.
Stupid, ugly things. I hate them.
I didn't even touch it.

"Scorpions are in the spider family."

I hate spiders. The way they kind of slink around and slip over the ground. They don't make any noise. It's like they float above it. Yuk. Now, I hate scorpions too. Stupid things.

Boston is still explaining. "They hide under leaves and in dark spots. Most are about two inches long, but two species can grow to three or four inches. They are black or dark brown and some are a tawny tan color. All have a stinger on their tail."

No kidding.

"Some scorpion stings are lethal. Their venom can kill people and animals. We don't have any of those here in Florida, though their sting might be bad for an ill person or a child, or someone with an allergic reaction. I'll look that up."

She's always looking things up.

Then she kind of laughs. "Of course, I guess the pain is exceedingly agonizing and you might wish you were dead."

You think? I move my paw cautiously again.

She's still in her lecture mode. "I think that was a bark scorpion."

Bark? Like a dog?

"I'm not sure how they got that name. But that's what I think from my quick look. Light colored legs, dark brown with yellow dashes on its back. They're nocturnal mostly, he was probably sleeping under that leaf. They have little hairs on their body for sensing vibrations, like the whiskers on your legs. He felt you coming. And he struck. Scorpions are carnivores, which means they like meat. They crush prey with their claws. You might not have noticed they have claws in front, like a crab."

Scorpion

I hadn't. I'm warm in her lap, and her soft voice comforts me. My sleepy eyelids close and I fall asleep.

Rattling in the kitchen wakes me up. I'm by myself curled in the chair and Boston is cooking in the kitchen. She's talking to herself.

I like to be nearby when she's cooking because she shares morsels. I stand and stagger. *Ow.*

No. Not ow. My paw doesn't hurt. The mitten on my foot tripped me. I examine it. Flex my toes. Shake my foot to get the bandage off. It doesn't budge.

I lick it. Nip. Bite. Tug. It's on tight.

I curl my paw and pull the bandage from the tip of my toes and slip it off with some fur attached to the tape.

"Stop. Tiger."

I shake the white stuff off. Scattering it like snowflakes.

Boston grabs my paw. "No. Don't shake that stuff all over the chair. Let me do it."

She gently brushes it off my foot and examines it closely. Looks it over. Leans down real quick and kisses it. "All better. You're cleared for take-off. Come help me get ready for the BBQ." She brushes all the loose flakes from the chair into her hand and heads back to the kitchen, but I lick my paw clean before I follow. I find a little bump where that nasty thing stung me, but that's all. Time to go check out the food.

"The men are cooking tonight." She snorts. "That means that they stand around the BBQ, turn the meat, talk, and drink beer. The women do all the work. We prepare everything else." She repeats herself. "Yeah, the men are cooking dinner. We butter and wrap the corn in tinfoil. Same with baked potatoes, onions, and buns.

We bring the condiments. But, I guess it's a good trade off. It gives us a good excuse to get together and gossip. Maybe Pam will bring her famous peanut-butter cake. I just think it's humorous when we say the men are cooking. I get a boot out of it."

She doesn't mean a boot like someone kicking a cat. She's means it's funny. "Right. They're cooking dinner."

She laughs. "Well, at least since we each get to cook what we like, all the food is good." Boston has her preparation process down to a science; she's making potato salad, stuffed eggs, and two cakes. Other folks will bring the macaroni salad and coleslaw, or slice tomatoes and wash lettuce for the hamburgers, chop onions and kraut for the hot dogs. Some guys bring a bag of chips or a six pack of beer.

While she boils the eggs and potatoes, she chops celery and onions for the potato salad. "We're making extra today, because we always seem to run out."

We? She means she is doing the work, I supervise. I'm the taste tester and eat the extras.

She turns on the oven and mixes the batter for the cakes and pours it into the Bundt pans which she puts into the oven. Next, she mixes together the mayonnaise and seasonings for the potato salad in a huge bowl.

And puts a dollop of the mayonnaise in my food dish. *Yay*. My reward.

She puts the eggs on the counter top to cool and I keep an eye on them for her. In case one rolls off. None do.

She peels them, cuts the eggs in half and scoops out

the yellow, saving a little out to put in my dish. Then adds mayonnaise and deviled ham to her mound.

I get a dollop of both of those too. The deviled ham is kind of a paste and sort of tastes like ham. I don't know where the devil part comes in. It's salty, but that's okay.

She finishes the stuffed eggs and gives me a smidgeon of leftover deviled ham mixed with egg yolk.

Yay.

She takes the cakes out of the oven to cool. She doesn't ever frost them, says she doesn't know how to make frosting.

I'm not sure what frosting is, back home it was cold and snow.

"Party Time," Kevlar hollers as he turns on the sparkle lights, and one of the guys pulls his vehicle close for music. Beers are opened, and the grill is started. The grill is a monster. Kevlar and Bob built it, welding together two old oil drums cut lengthwise. Only the bottoms are welded together, the tops are hinged and open separately.

Boston carries her food out, and I follow and take up a position near the meat. I like to hang near the burgers and keep an eye on the menfolk. Their cooking is nowhere near as organized as Boston's and sometimes they get a little rambunctious. When no one is looking, I'll score some beef.

I sit comfortably, watching, listening, waiting. Hunting a burger. Patient.

Motion by that rock. Something moved. I pin the spot with ears pointed. Wait.

A scorpion.

Ugh. Not two in one day. It isn't the same one which stung me. This one is bigger, darker.

My upper lip curls.

It thinks I can't see it in the dusk. Can't see it's ugly pincers and its gross pointed, segmented tail.

It skitters across the pavement staying in the shadows.

I tuck my paw under me. I haven't forgotten the burning.

I hate scorpions. Hate them.

Stupid things.

It edges closer and my muscles tense.

It's ignoring me. Acting as if it doesn't see me. Maybe it doesn't.

It creeps, slinks, whatever it is they do, toward us. I almost edge back as it climbs onto the baby's blanket. Jeffy's blanket.

It skitters toward Jeffy. On purpose? Or is it aiming for me? Do I care if it stings Jeffy?

I'm not overly fond of him. Always has drool down his chin and a soggy cookie in his hand. He's an uncoordinated little guy. All awkward and clumsy. He doesn't walk or stand on two feet, but scrambles around on all four like me and even on all fours, he tends to tumble over. One time he flung his arm out and shot soggy cookie drool at me. It hardened like cement in my fur.

And he smells. Always. Either of that stuff they call baby powder (not made from babies, but for babies) or baby poop (made by babies). Sometimes both. In spite of that, all the women gush over him.

Not that I'm jealous.

Boston helped him pat me once. She held his hand and guided it to stroke my fur. Sticky, gooey hand. Yuk. Took me forever to get my fur clean and his stink off.

The scorpion heads straight for Jeffy.

I squint at it and flatten my ears. A snarl starts in the back of my throat.

The scorpion waves his claws like a crab and arches its tail over its back. The stinger points forward.

Hate them. Hate it.

Jeffy leans toward it, reaching out.

Stop. Don't.

No! No! No! No!

I'm not screaming at the scorpion. I can't stop him.

I'm not yelling at the kid. He's already tumbling toward the scorpion.

No. I'm yelling at myself.

Don't jump. Don't pounce. He'll sting again. It will hurt. It will burn. Stay away from it.

But it's too late.

I've launched myself before I think the last no.

Time slows. Sound stops.

I'm aiming to land behind and on top of the creature. Behind the barb.

But Jeffy, falling, hits me. Slams me with his soggy cookie hand. Knocks me out of the air. He falls to the side.

I land in front of the scorpion. Not behind.

Sound comes back.

Catfish hollering. "The cat's attacking the baby. The cat's attacking Johnny."

Time speeds up and the barbed tail, pointing right between my eyes, stabs forward.

Don't sting me. Don't sting me.

I swipe at the scorpion and smack it as it strikes. Snatch my head back out of the way. Feel the stinger brush past my ear. Hear it.

I wallop it hard with my paw. Give it a double bash. Whack it. Then smash it with both paws. Smack it again.

Hate it. Hate it.

I'm lunging forward to chomp it in half when I'm grabbed from behind and lifted off my feet.

What?

"Rrrrr. Snarl. Hiss."

Ranger Bob has me. I smell his aftershave. He holds me in the air, away from his body, the way I've seen him do Wolf, his own cat, when Wolf is angry and in attack mode.

I struggle but can't reach his hands.

Suddenly there is commotion all around. People charging toward us.

"He attacked Johnny," Catfish yells. "I saw him attack the baby."

"No." Boston says, racing up. "Tiger didn't." She reaches for me.

"I saw him," Catfish yells.

Ranger Bob hands me to Boston and I've calmed

down enough to let her pull me to her chest and curl an arm under me.

Catfish pushes in and reaches for me. She steps away from him.

I snarl at him and shrink into the safety of her arms.

"Give that animal to me," he growls. "I'm putting it down."

Put me down? No, I want Boston.

"He didn't hurt Jeffy," Boston insists.

Catfish yells, gloating. "I saw him. He attacked the baby. None of you can deny it this time. You all saw him. He jumped on Johnny. Knocked him down. That animal is a menace. I'll break his neck."

Break my neck? Because the baby whacked me with his cookie? I glare at him. Wish him turned into a cockroach. My fur stands up and I growl at him in warning.

Kevlar's calm voice silences everyone. "Hold your horses, Stewart. Don't get so excited. Better take another look. You might have misread the situation"

Catfish rounds on him, his face an ugly scowl and his fists clenched. "I'm putting that animal down. I don't care what you say. I saw him tackle the baby. He's a menace."

Kevlar heaves a heavy sigh and shakes his head. "Take another look at the dangerous cat." He points at me. "Look at his paws."

"Yeah. Look at his paws," Ranger Bob says in a tone close to amazement.

Catfish turns.

We both look.

Yuk.

The stupid scorpion is clutched in my paws, crushed and mangled and dangling. Squashed, torn, and punctured. Dead. Very gratifyingly dead.

I look up at Catfish in amazement.

Tiger Looking at Scorpion

Scorpion

Tiger in Surprise

I did that? Guess I showed it.

Kevlar pulls the scorpion off with his cooking tongs and holds it up for everyone to see.

Bob says, "A scorpion that size might have killed Jeffy. Jeffy. The kid's name is Jeffy. Not Johnny, Stewart."

Boston hugs me close to her and I cling to her.

Kevlar says, "Tiger wasn't attacking Jeffy. He was protecting him."

Jeffy's Mom comes over and reaches out tentatively to give me a pat with her free hand. She has the kid in the other.

Ranger Bob says, "Excitement's over; let's get back to the food," and he herds folks back to the picnic tables and cooker.

Catfish is left by himself, frowning and gritting his teeth.

Huh. So there.

Kevlar pats me, wiping off the soggy cookie. "Tiger, you sure destroyed that scorpion. I'm going to cook you your very own hamburger."

A hamburger? My own?

I hope he isn't going to use those scorpion tongs on it. Ick.

He sterilizes them in the flames. Good.

I twist around to watch him pick up a burger and throw it on the grill.

Boston says, "Tiger likes his hamburger just hot on the inside, light brown on the outside, leaking grease."

"Really?" Kevlar studies both of us.

I do? Yeah, really. Leaking grease.

Boston shrugs a shoulder. "I don't have a clue. But if he doesn't, he should."

Kevlar snorts, but flips the unseasoned patty. "I can do that."

I hadn't meant to save the kid. It was an accident. My leap had been instinctive. But I won't tell anyone. And maybe someone will give me a stuffed egg. My favorite.

KILLER

K EVLAR'S HUNTING.
I know. People don't hunt, but that's what he's doing. Hunting. Kevlar calls it fishing. He reads the water with his eyes, searching the surface for the rippling telltale sign of bait fish. He walks slowly along the shoreline holding the cast net. The net is round, about six feet across with lead weights along the outer edge. A line stretches from each weight to the main cord at the center. He's holding the outer edge weights gathered in his hands and has the line wrapped around his wrist.

He stops, staring at an area where the surface is disturbed. A school of small mullet are just below the surface making small ripples and swells with their swirling fins and tails. He continues along the shore slightly ahead of the school and adjusts the edges of his cast net, grasping the weights in his outstretched hands. He stands sideways, watching, waiting. Patient. Waiting for the right moment to pounce. He moves one foot forward and casts the net.

It flares and spreads wide into a full circle as it sails across the water and then drops over the ruffled area. The lead weights take it to the bottom, trapping the fish under it.

A perfect cast. He has captured the quarry.

He tugs the central lines gathering the attached weights together at the base of the net and then tugs harder and pulls the net out of the water with the fish inside. Water streams out and the bait mullet wiggle, flip, and flop. Each is about three inches long and shiny and silver. Kevlar uses the bait fish to catch big fish for supper. He carries his catch to the dock where Boston and I are waiting and dumps the fish into the bait bucket, shaking out the net.

I stay close because sometimes a fish misses the bucket and flops onto the dock and I can snatch it. I'm ready to pounce, but none escape.

Oh well.

Kevlar grabs two fish out of the bucket, handing one to Boston, and then lowers the bucket into the water after tying it securely to a cleat. The bucket has holes in it for water to pass through and keep the bait fish alive. He threads his fish onto his hook and casts it out into the water where the fish swims around, hopefully attracting a bigger fish. Boston does the same. Then he puts his rod into the pole holder attached to the dock pilings and sits on the bench to wait for the pole tip to bend signaling he has a big fish on his line. When that happens, he'll jump up and reel in supper.

Kevlar always catches fish. Always. We never go

home empty handed. And I always get a share, before he batters it and cooks it, frying it in grease. Grease is good. Batter means rolling it in some kind of meal or flour. Not slapping it around with a paw. I prefer my fish unbattered, and Kevlar always saves some for me. But I can eat it battered and fried, too.

Boston says, "I've heard good things about the new ranger from Rainer who's due in on Monday."

I'm not interested and lean over the edge of the dock to bat at the crabs climbing the pilings. They're not good to eat, but they're entertaining because they act as if they have no idea where they've been or where they're going, frequently just walking around in circles waving their claws at nothing. Kind of like the lubber grasshoppers.

"Yo. Hey," someone hollers from the residence area, and we all turn.

A guy is jogging toward us carrying a tan bundle, a woman is walking behind at a more sedate pace.

Boston and Kevlar stand when the man steps on the dock holding the bundle in one arm and extends his hand in the greeting humans use instead of sniffing.

I watch suspiciously.

The man says in a friendly, but extra loud voice, "I'm Jackson Holding, the new ranger." He nods over his shoulder at the woman approaching. "My wife, Kate. She'll be working for Resource Management."

The guy smells a little weird; it's what he's carrying. Otherwise the people smell okay. Kind of fresh and natural, clean and outdoorsy. I look closer at the bundle, it smells like a dog. Hard to mistake the smell now, or the shape. It whines, and he sets it down on the dock. It stands. A dog, young dog, but not a puppy. It has a long muzzle with a long pink tongue hanging out. Long ears hanging down. He prances, his tail whipping around back and forth furiously in typical giddy dog fashion. I can only shake my head at its uncontrolled excitement.

Killer

Kevlar introduces himself and Boston. "We were expecting you Monday," he says, "but we have the apartment ready if you're planning to move in now."

"No," Jackson says. "We're staying in town with

friends over the weekend and just came for a look-see, to check out the visitor center and campground. Meet the people. Folks told us you two were down here fishing. Nice spot."

"Yeah. Perk of the required housing. Who's this cute guy?" Kevlar asks nodding to the dog.

"My son. Killer."

Huh. Killer? The dog is small, not just young. About my size. A bit larger. Of course, I'm pretty large for a cat. Maine Coon cats come in large.

I walk over to introduce myself and tell him who's boss, after puffing up my fur to make myself a tad bigger.

The dog freezes when he sees me, and I stare hard with squinted eyes.

"Killer?" Kevlar says and gives the dog a pat.

I turn my narrow-eyed stare on Kevlar for patting the stranger, but he ignores me.

Jackson says with a note of pride, "Toss him a chew bone, you'll see. Or an old shoe, or even a new shoe; he'll destroy it in a minute."

New shoes? He destroys new shoes? Hmmm. Anyone who destroys shoes deserves some admiration. Later, maybe, for now I'm in his face. Well, two feet away. I sniff and show him my canines. (Who ever named cat teeth, canines?) I move my ears to point slightly out to the side.

He smells like a happy dog.

His tail makes a half jerk. Uncertain. His eyes are wide open and his ears half-cocked. One ear twitches.

I lay mine half back and narrow the squint. Flick my tail once.

He's not impressed with my squint and puts his tongue in his mouth and grins. Wags his tail.

The people are silent, watching, probably ready to intervene.

Both his ears twitch.

I show a little more of my eye teeth.

He grins wider, leans down and bows on his front paws in invitation, his tongue hanging out. His back-end wiggles once and he abruptly about-faces and takes off running.

I'm after him in a heartbeat.

Huh?

I chase him off the dock, across the field, and around the picnic table.

He makes a sudden reversal. Me too. Now he's dogging me; his nose almost pushing the tip of my out-stretched tail. I lead him around the sea grapes, the rosebush, and then it's my turn to about-face and chase him.

He dashes around the squad car and races back to the dock. The women jump out of the way, and he rushes to Jackson, stops abruptly, and falls down and rolls over on his back with his feet in the air.

Takes me by surprise and I skid around him and manage to stop three steps farther along. I turn and frown at him and then decide to lick my back leg.

See, everyone, I planned the skid.

Licking my leg lets me hide my smile. That was kind

of fun. It's been a long time since I've played chase. I can't believe I played chase with a dog. Really?

And people saw me do it. Play with a dog. They're staring. Mouths open. Guess they can't believe it either.

I'm a little surprised myself. I'm going to pretend it never happened, but I grin as I lick my leg again.

Boston breaks the silence. "Well. I guess they get along."

Kevlar says in that dry tone of his, "I've never seen that cat move so fast. Unless someone was calling him for dinner."

What? Now that is just mean. I give him my look reserved for a stupid mouse. Boston snorts at him and introduces me. "That's Tiger," she says.

Jackson smiles and reaches down intending to pat my head. "What a sweet kitty."

"Stop," Kevlar warns sharply. "Don't."

I show Jackson all my teeth. He jumps back and pulls his hand close to his body.

Kevlar laughs. "That's our Tiger. Unfriendly. Doesn't like to be touched. And he probably prefers words like strong or fast as opposed to sweet and kitty."

That's more like it, Kevlar. No one calls me kitty.

"I think he thinks of himself as a Maine Coon cat," Boston says.

Thinks of myself as? I am a Maine Coon cat. Just a smaller version. With no ear tufts.

Jackson turns to me with both his hands safe in his jeans pockets. "You are a remarkably fast cat."

Okay. That's better. Sucking up big time. Smart man.

Boston returns to the original conversation. "You're moving in Monday?"

"Yeah." Jackson says absently, watching Kevlar pull his fishing pole from its holder, and reel it in.

"What are you fishing for?"

"Redfish or snook. They move through on the turn of the high tide." Kevlar checks his bait.

"What's that you're using for bait?"

"Mullet." He shows Jackson the fish on the end of the hook and casts it back out "Catch 'em with that net," he points to the net laid out ready for another cast. Kevlar checks the other pole.

"So, you just cast out the bait and sit here and wait?" Kate asks.

Kevlar shakes his head. "Nope. Not that simple. Have to watch the pole. Have to be ready to jump up if the tip bends. Have to drink a beer." He motions to the cooler. "Help yourself. Sodas and water in there too."

Jackson and Kate select water and sit on the bench where they all talk. Their equivalent to sniffing and circling. Kate asks local questions which Boston answers succinctly. "Publix is the best grocery store. Car registration and license is Homestead which is Dade county. Voter registration is Key West which is Monroe County about one hundred miles south after you get out of the park. And, just to make things interesting," Boston says, "our land-line is out of Everglades City in Collier County." Then the conversation moves on to "What parks have you worked at?" Boston asks. And based on that reply, they'll see if they know any of the same people. Park Service is small and they always find someone both parties know.

I don't really care about all that, so I watch the dog. Sluggo. He wants me to call him, Sluggo. He sniffs all the posts on the dock, meandering around with his nose down nearly touching the ground. He wanders off the dock and sniffs around the mangroves, careful to keep his feet dry while peeing on the low branches. He's such a dog. He works his way along the shoreline parallel to the dock. Sniffing and peeing. What dogs live for.

I move to the shore side of the dock, curious how many times the animal can pee. Not that I'm counting.

A reel sings and I turn to see the tip of Kevlar's pole dip toward the horizon. He stands and snatches it from its holder. The others crowd around to watch the spot where the line cuts the water.

Kevlar lets the tip of the pole follow the fish, keeping some pressure on the reel, holding the pole up, letting the fish run. That's the action I watch, not the line. Who cares where the stupid line enters the water. I'm smarter than that. I watch the man, the skilled hunter. He feels the fish's actions transmitted through the line and pole to his hands, senses where the fish is going next. The hunter plays out some line to let the fish run, letting it lead. He pulls back on the pole, tightens the line, and brings the fish back. Repeats the process until the fish is worn-out.

The tail breaks the surface in a swirl, a sure sign of exhaustion, and I can see the black spot. Redfish.

Jackson yells in excitement. Boston gets the dip net ready. Kevlar lets the redfish run one more time for freedom and then easily reels it in to the dock where Boston expertly slips the net under it and lifts it out of the water. She twists the net one time making sure the fish is secure and lays it on the dock. My people work well together. Smooth and slick.

Sluggo doesn't come back to watch.

What's he up to? I turn around. He's busy with something. I hear the rustle at the same time his ears prick up and he points, nose first, at the sound. I focus on the spot. Snake. Brown. Murky pattern bands, yellow stripe above a dark stripe running behind the eye to the back of its head. Slithering through the grass and leaves.

Sluggo moves closer to it with an excited wiggle.

The snake raises its head. Triangular head. Boston says that means a venomous snake.

Oh, oh. Sluggo. Back off.

The snake opens its mouth wide and with a long sharp hiss shows its fangs. A white mouth. Wide white mouth.

Cottonmouth. Water moccasin. Boston showed me his picture. "Deadly," she said. "Poisonous. Stay away from them."

Sluggo moves a step closer, wiggling his hips, ready to pounce.

"**Merooww!**" *Back off!* I scream a warning, a mixture of roar and snarl.

My yell stops Sluggo a moment. The people turn to look, first at me, then at Sluggo.

Killer

"Cottonmouth," Kevlar says, moving quickly.

"**Yowrrrll**!" I scream again at the stupid dog. *Move away. Move back.*

Sluggo jerks his head toward me and gives me a wide grin which says, "He's mine. I found him. I got him. You're too far away to stop me."

Looks back to the snake.

"Killer," Jackson hollers. "No. Stop."

The dog wiggles his back end.

I hear a scrape on the dock. The cast net whooshes as it flies over my head.

It doesn't open all the way into the full circle. Doesn't flare. Only opens an uneven odd two-foot shape and drops over the dog with a loud WHOMP.

Wow, Kevlar.

Sluggo yelps in surprise, pinned flat to the ground by the weighted net. He can't move. The snake pulls its head back. The lead weights almost clipped its nose. It sniffs with its tongue one time. Out, in. Then he turns and glides quickly back into the water to disappear.

Suddenly everyone is talking at once as they race to the dog. Everyone except Boston who picks me up to cuddle. "You are such a smart brave cat. You saved Killer. I am so proud of you."

Well, of course I saved the dumb dog. Someone had to.

Kevlar checks the shoreline to make sure the snake is gone and then grabs the weights and lifts the cast net off Sluggo.

"Cottonmouth?" Jackson asks cradling his dog. "Is that what you said?"

"Yeah. Water moccasin or cottonmouth. We also have the Eastern Diamondback rattler and the pygmy rattler. The animals learn to stay away from them."

"Wow. I need a beer after that," Jackson says and grabs one before collapsing on the bench with the dog in his lap.

I should get a shrimp or something. I am a smart and brave cat. I saved the dog. Well maybe I had a little help from Kevlar.

"You'll show me how to throw one of those net things, right?" Jackson asks Kevlar.

"Sure." He lays out the cast net ready for the next toss.

Boston exchanges a look with Kevlar and gets a nod. "Plenty of fish here," she says. "You two want to come to dinner? Kevlar will clean it and fry it up along with some hushpuppies. I'll slice up some avocados and make a salad."

Jackson checks with Kate. "We'd like that," he says. "Even though I'm not sure what a hushpuppy is. Is it a local food? We're from Mt. Rainer and New Jersey. It's not a dog, is it? Or an almost snake-bit dog?"

Kevlar laughs. "Not dog. You'll like them."

"In that case, we're game. No one is expecting us for supper. I have some nice wine in the car."

I don't like hushpuppies. Kevlar puts onions and peppers in them. I check the fish. Looks like maybe enough for four people and one Maine Coon cat. One hero Maine Coon cat.

Killer

Killer and Tiger

KILLER SEQUEL

I'M HALF ASLEEP. Lying in the warm afternoon sun, the crisp grass under my back, a soft breeze ruffling my belly fur, cooling my skin. Ah, yes. This is the life. My daily routine. It doesn't get much better than this. I'm dreaming with the warm sun on my belly.

My paw twitches. All four legs are up in the air with my front paw tips bent and hanging down limp, and I probably look like a dead bird instead of the strong, tough Maine Coon cat I am. But I'm too comfortable to worry about appearances.

Besides, Boston is the only one around to see. She came out with me and is either reading or painting. Don't know which and am not opening an eye to check, but she brought two books and her canvas, easel, and painting supplies. Whatever.

Ah, sun, breeze, quiet.

Well, quiet except for the grackles crackling. They're songbirds.

Ha. Songbirds? Their noisy coughs and squeaking are never pleasant-sounding and seem to be extra loud and grating this morning. Boston says their call is disk-or-dent, she spelled it as discordant, which Boston says means the opposite of song. Sometimes she calls the noise, ca-ca-fon-y. Spelled cacophony. The grackles are black all over. Well, actually, like the redwings which do sing, the black color is glossy on the males and dull brownish on the females. Anyhow they're gathered under the trees chirruping tweeting and rummaging for seeds and maybe small frogs. More disturbing than the redwings. Far enough away that I don't feel a need to hunt, but almost want to get up and walk over there and slap one in the head.

Almost. I'm going to ignore them.

Just lie here, lazily.

Yawn.

Oops, that almost woke me up. I wiggle my shoulders to scratch an itch. Lazy never felt so good.

There is some squawking and chattering on the park radio, too. But I'm only half listening. It's a background drone. White noise.

I zone out. Enjoying the warm, the quiet, the breeze. It's a perfect day to lie on my back, in the cool grass, my paws in the air. Bliss.

Wait.

Sniff. Sniff? Beef? Is that beef? I take a deep breath. Beef. My favorite. I open an eye. Beef beats sun any day. Both eyes. Sniff. I look up at our apartment. I remember. Boston's cooking beef. She put it in the oven before we came out. Maybe it's time to eat. I roll over and sit up to look at her.

Jackson opens his door and doggy claws click on the porch and clatter down the steps and then Sluggo is in my face. Only long enough for a smile and a tail wag and then he's off to pee.

Jackson hollers, "Yo. Hey," from the porch and comes down the stairs. "Something smells awful good," he says.

"Supper. New beef recipe. Want to come over and eat with us tonight?"

"Love to. Happy you took the hint. Thank you."

Sluggo is sniffing around. As if anything has changed since he sniffed everything the last time he was out. But he's a dog. That's what they do.

He finally finds the perfect spot and pees. But like I said, he's a dog so he keeps sniffing until he finds another place to pee. And another. And another. He seems to have an endless supply of pee.

He doesn't seem to need a special spot to poop and he proves it. No sniffing. Just walks around, suddenly squats, poops, and moves on.

Stupid dog. Leaves his poop anywhere.

Cats pee and poop in one spot. And yes, I do like to pick the perfect spot and spend some time selecting it. Then I dig a nice hole, poop delicately into it, and cover it up. Cats don't leave poop out for people to stumble over.

Jackson sighs and, grumbling, grabs a shovel and scoops the poop up and drops it in the rubbish.

Kevlar drives in and Jackson complains, "Joe told me,

and I quote, *ain't picking up garbage with poop in it.* Can't you do something, Kev? He works for you. You're his boss. I mean, come on, tell him to pick up my garbage."

I like Joe. He's huge, but sweet, and he always has a treat for me. He collects the garbage twice a week. He might be only the guy who picks up the garbage, but the way he sees it, he's the most important person in the park. *Because he picks up the garbage.* Without him, everything would stop. Truth.

He wields a lot of power and everyone kind of does what he says. Even Boston. Joe had a similar discussion about poop with her a long time ago. She keeps my litter box by the toilet for easy poop disposal.

Jackson continues his complaint. "Irritates me to have to pick this poop up, irritates me more Joe refuses to pick up my garbage when I put the poop in it. I can understand why I have to pick the poop up, but why can't I drop it in the garbage can. Come on. What am I supposed to do?" he whines.

Kevlar studies the garbage can a moment and responds in a slow drawl. "I was hoping you and Joe could work it out without getting me involved."

Jackson crosses his arms in front of his chest.

Kevlar shrugs. "Okay. Let's start with your neighbors. I've been noticing that there's a problem with your rubbish can. It stinks of dog poop. It stinks ten minutes after you put the poop in it and then for two, three more days until the garbage pick-up. Your neighbors are irritated by the smell. I make a wide berth around it to get to my vehicle.

By the time Joe has to empty it, he finds your garbage too offensive to pick up. You with me so far?"

Kevlar waits for Jackson to nod.

"Part of your responsibility as a dog owner is the proper disposal of his excrement. We all appreciate you picking up the poop so we don't walk in it, but you need to take an additional step. We are all offended by the odor which permeates the housing area. You know, if you complain to me officially, I have to write up a report and you are not going to look very good, you'll stink worse than the poop. Do you really want me to do that? Officially?"

"Okay. Okay. What do you suggest?"

"Put the dog poop in a plastic poop sack, one of those dog waste-bags. It won't smell. Your neighbors will be happy, and Joe will do his job. Buy some dog waste sacks. Meanwhile, borrow some from Johnson. He solved this same problem months ago."

Johnson has a little tiny dog. His poop fits in the finger part of a rubber glove.

The background radio chatters turn into real words and the two men pause in their discussion to listen.

"550. 786." The ranger station is 786, they're calling the district ranger, 550. They use numbers over the radio instead of names. Not sure why. When there is no answer they repeat the call a moment later. "550. 786."

Bob responds. "551."

"Catfish must be out of contact," Jackson says.

The ranger station says, "Bob. Visitors report wild dogs at Nine Mile Pond harassing the wildlife."

"Wild dogs? That's a new one. How long ago, 786?"

"Forty-five minutes."

"Okay. I'm enroute. Be about ten minutes, I'm near Pa-hay-okee."

The radio goes silent and Jackson caves. "Okay. Okay. No reports. I'll get some poop sacks."

"Good man," Kevlar says and walks over to give Boston a hug and look at her painting, then walks back to sit with Sluggo and Jackson on the steps.

I close my eyes and go back to sleep.

A few minutes later, the radio chatter disturbs me, and I open an eye. Jackson and Kevlar are still gossiping on the stairs.

"786. 551. No dogs here now."

"Just received a report the dogs are at West Lake."

"Long ways for wild dogs to travel," Bob says.

"551. 786. These folks say the dogs were in a car with two men. No descriptions."

"Enroute. 551"

The ranger station continues. "The visitors say they saw two men with two dogs at West Lake. The men were tossing a box turtle back and forth, playing keep away from their dogs. The visitors came right here to report it. Fifteen, twenty minutes ago. Car is an old red Explorer."

"Thanks. 551."

Suddenly an engine revs and a red car speeds down the road, races across the field, and stops with a squeal by the shore. The doors fly open and two men and two big dogs pile out in a loud tangle of drunken laughter.

Killer Sequel

Hmm. I open both eyes now. Jackson takes out his radio and informs both 786 and Bob that the dogs are in the restricted residential area.

One of the men tosses something to the bigger dog, a black one, which catches it in the air and races off in our direction. The brown dog chases it. The black dog stops and turns and drops the thing on the ground. It falls with a thunk and doesn't move.

I point my ears forward for a better look. Raise my nose to catch a sniff. And that fractional movement catches the black dog's attention. He jerks his head in my direction, his beady black eyes staring directly at me.

Two Dogs

Sluggo makes a step toward the dogs and the big black head examines him and dismisses the small dog. He stares back at me.

Charges. Like a freight train.

I don't have time to stand, let alone run or sidestep. He's on me as I roll over and try to get to my feet.

His open mouth drowns me with bad breath. I look past all the gleaming white teeth down his throat.

Jackson and Kevlar jump up.

Boston hollers, "Tiger."

I swipe his muzzle with all my claws. Connect and draw blood.

Startled, he snaps his jaws shut barely missing me and shakes his head, tossing blood.

But he has me boxed in and, with white teeth, all sharp and pointy, he lunges again.

Sluggo growls and with hackles raised he attacks the dog. Clamps his small teeth on a back leg.

The black dog hesitates and tries to shake the little dog off.

Sluggo has given me a precious second. I leap straight up, the only direction I can move, and land on the top of the dog's head and grab hold. My front claws dig in deep above the eyes, back claws clawing the sides of its muzzle.

I bite hard on his ear. My teeth meet.

He raises his head and hollers.

Whips his head from side to side.

I grip tighter, claw deeper.

Kevlar charges.

Jackson too, yelling into his radio, calling for reinforcements.

The dog whips violently around, and I'm thrown off. To hit the ground hard, roll three times, and smash against a sea grape trunk.

Dazed.

Alive.

The animal twists around and grabs Sluggo. Pulls him off. Shakes him. Tosses him carelessly away to land with a sharp crack on the pavement. Where he lies still.

"God damn, God damn," Jackson screams. "My dog."

I try to get up before the dog remembers me.

Then Kevlar is between us.

It growls at him. Snaps at him.

Kevlar punches the dog in the mouth.

Hah.

Jackson has his stun gun out of its holster. He shoves it into the dog's shoulder, behind its neck, and squeezes the trigger.

There's a pop, a bright flash, and a sizzling crackling high-pitched noise.

The dog shudders and falls to the ground. Convulses.

The shudders seem to go on forever, but the dog finally lies still.

It's over.

I take a deep breath and struggle to my feet a little shaky.

Jackson is shaking too. He holsters the gun. "Didn't want to do that. These Tasers can kill a dog."

He glances quickly over at Sluggo. Grimaces. Pulls those plastic twist-tie things out of his pocket and wraps them around the dog's front feet. Kevlar shoves a thick dowel into the dog's mouth, crosswise, and wraps silver tape around and around the muzzle anchoring the stick to prop the mouth open with the tongue hanging out.

I limp over to Sluggo who is still lying motionless where he landed. Sniff him.

I lick his head, just below his eye where there is a spot of blood.

Not his blood.

Boston kneels beside us, picks me up. "You okay Tiger?" she asks. "You okay? Anything broken?" She's in her first aid mode and feels me all over. When she finishes, satisfied I'm okay, she turns to Sluggo.

"Oh, Killer. Come on puppy. Look at me."

Jackson bends over and uses another twist-tie on the dog's back legs. Then he and Kevlar tie the front feet to the back and the animal is truly trussed.

Boston gently feels Sluggo, talking softly. "Nothing broken. Let me check the bites."

I get down and lick his eye. The lid flutters.

"Can you wag your tail, Puppy? Is your back okay?" Boston asks and lifts the tip.

I lick again and this time the eye opens and stays open and the tail wags once feebly.

Boston murmurs, "Oh, Killer. Such a brave, fierce dog."

He is. He is brave and fierce. The silly little dog attacked that giant dog. To protect me. He saved me from all the sharp white teeth.

Sluggo smiles, pants, but stays down.

Jackson drops to his knees and looks to Boston.

"He's okay. Nothing broken, cuts are superficial," she says.

Sluggo struggles part way up and Jackson hugs him close sighing with relief.

"I thought he was dead."

"He saved Tiger," Boston says. "Did you see that? He attacked that dog and saved Tiger."

I nudge her chin.

"Brave Tiger," she says and pats my head.

Yes. I'm brave too.

Kevlar walks over. "Tiger about tore that ear in half. Gonna need stitching. Never seen a cat do anything like that. Jump on a dog's head." He shrugs.

"Brave dog, too." He looks at Sluggo. "Actually, attacked that dog to save the cat. He deserves a big steak."

Me too. I deserve a steak. He wouldn't be a hero if it wasn't for me.

We're gathered like that. Me in Boston's arms, Sluggo in Jackson's, Kevlar leaning over us, a hand on Boston's shoulder. Aftershock. Drawing strength from each other. I'm not the only one feeling weak.

The two drunks are still wading in the bay, laughing and splashing, falling down drunkenly, trying to entice the brown dog into the water. It's running up and down the bank, barking excitedly, but each time it gets near the edge, it backs off.

Two squad cars scream into the residence area and stop next to the red car. Four rangers jump out. A maintenance truck rolls up behind.

If I felt stronger, I'd walk over and supervise, but my legs are still a little shaky. I can watch from here.

Shorty gets out of the truck and pulls out a long pole with a loop on the end. He walks toward the dog.

"What's that pole?" Jackson asks Kevlar.

"That's a catch-pole with a spring-loaded noose on the end."

"How come a maintenance guy has the catch pole and not a ranger?"

"Shorty was an animal control officer before he came here. He helps the research guys when they have to trap a wounded or sick animal. He's our expert. Watch."

The dog is so focused on the men in the water, he doesn't hear Shorty come up behind him. One of the drunks' yells, "Look out, King, look out." But the dog doesn't understand and continues barking and jumping.

Shorty misses on his first pass, but easily slips the noose over the dog's head on his second try. He pulls the noose tight and yanks the animal back a step.

The dog turns quickly toward Shorty, but the pole keeps him out of bite range, and Shorty drags the animal to the back of the truck where one of the rangers has a cage open on the ground. Using the pole, Shorty pushes the growling dog into it and slams the door shut, locks it and disengages the noose.

Together the men lift the cage into the pick-up bed.

The laughing, hooting men are not so easily managed, and two rangers wade into the water after them. The drunks play keep away, kind of like Sluggo when Jackson wants him to come and Sluggo wants to go. The rangers drag the men out of the water, make them sit on the grass and handcuff them. Then they search the car. They pull items out and put them aside.

One of the squad cars leaves and Bob walks over to us. "You guys all okay?"

Jackson checks with Boston and she nods. "Yeah. Yeah, we are."

I tuck my head under Boston's chin.

Jackson rubs a hand over his face, the other hand resting on Sluggo. He nods to the black dog. "Get that thing out of here. Can Shorty check its ear? Not the damn dog's fault it's running wild."

"I sent for another cage and Shorty's coming with the truck." He turns to Kevlar. "Kev, those men are drunk and we're all wet and I don't really want to get in the squad car like this. Can you help?"

Kevlar nods. "Sure, there are some tarps in my truck, you can throw them over the seats."

Jackson stands up, still holding Sluggo. "Cite them for endangering wildlife; make sure you have statements from the visitors who saw them at Nine Mile and West Lake. Add being in a closed area. Off a marked path.

Down there by the water. Having unlicensed dogs and letting them run loose. Find out if the animals have had their shots. If not, add that charge too. We'll write out what we witnessed."

He looks at Kevlar, Boston. "Forget anything?"

Boston says, "That thing they tossed to the dog, was a turtle, not a toy. That should carry some weight."

"Cite them for that, too."

Bob writes it all down. "We found air plants in the back of the car, along with a box turtle and a 'leave only your footprints' park service sign. Both men also have outstanding warrants."

"Idiots," Jackson says. "Take 'em all to town. Put them in jail. Take the dogs to animal rescue. I'm taking my dog inside and giving him a raw steak."

Huh? Steak? That's my favorite.

Kevlar puts an arm around Jackson's shoulders. "Come to our place, bring Killer. Boston has a hunk of beef we can all share. You can always give him the steak later."

Boston carries me inside.

Beef. My favorite.

BEGGAR LICE

WHAT THE HECK. *What was that?*
Something moved.

I study the spot. Give it a long look. Nothing.

I go back to work on my paw. Something is stuck to it. One of those dumb beggar lice seeds is stuck between the pads. Sticky stupid thing.

I try to grab it with my teeth.

Huh. There it is again. Something moved. I caught it out of the corner of my eye. Something. No noise, it's silent.

I examine the area, searching. Nothing. Hmm.

Back to my paw. A stupid little flat green bean is stuck to the hairs between my paw pads. It's shaped like a half circle with the top almost flat and the bottom squared off. About the size of a mouse eye. It's a seed and it sticks to stuff. Right now, this one is stuck on me.

They stick to everything that gets near them. Boston is idly picking some off her shoe. Muttering to herself.

She sees me watching and says, "Kev calls them stick-tights. I call them beggar lice."

Stick-tight is right. I finally get the stupid thing between my teeth and pull it off. Spit it out.

Oops.

Now it's stuck to my lip. I brush at it with a front paw and it transfers itself back to the paw.

Well, darn.

I shake my paw, but it sticks tight. *Hah.*

There's that movement again. This time I'm looking right at the spot and can zero in on it. I narrow my eyes to see better.

Leaves. Nothing. Just leaves. Little, wild grapevine leaves, that's all.

Huh?

They're moving. The leaves are creeping across the grass by the stairs. Weird. Leaves don't generally creep along the ground. There's no wind. I wander over for a closer look.

The leaves stop.

I sit and wait. I'm a cat. I wait well. Especially if food may be near.

The leaves move again. In a different direction.

Yup. Definitely weird. Leaves don't change direction and creep.

They stop moving. Start again and sort of stagger under the stairs behind the long blue planter with tall, dead, flower stalks. The stalks used to be tall green plants, lilies, Boston called them, but whatever they were, they're now tall dead sticks and don't offer much cover.

I edge around the planter.

The leafy vine thing shakes, and I point my ears at it and sniff. Sniff again. Smells like a bird. Not a songbird. I resniff. Hunter of some sort, has the smell of a meat eater. A bird for sure. I sink closer to the ground and edge forward on my belly.

If it is a bird, it's the strangest bird I've ever seen. All sort of green lumps, leaves, and a few feathers sticking out in odd directions. I think I can see a beak.

Yeah. A bird. I can make out a little bit of the head now in the shadow. From the beak and color, a kestrel.

Hidden Bird

It crawls awkwardly into some tall weeds hidden under the stairs of the stilt-house. I track its passage through them by the waving tops and walk into the weeds following along behind.

The weeds stink. I sniff.

There's something wrong with my whiskers. I test wiggle them.

Ouch.

Huh. They're stuck. I wiggle my nose.

Ooh.

I narrow my eyes. What? Now my sensor whiskers over my eyes are stuck to my forehead and tug my skin.

And the whiskers on the right side aren't working. I can't move them.

Something is tickling my ear. I twitch it. Still tickles. I shake my head. And suddenly, everything is worse. One eye is sort of stuck half open. Doesn't want to close. And the whiskers over that eye feel glued together. My shoulder itches. When I scratch it, something sticks to my paw. And down my leg.

What?

I move the eye that still works.

Beggar lice. On my paw. All down my front. I can feel them all over. I shake, twitch. Doesn't change anything.

I must have crawled through the stupid things.

Yikes. I see them all around through my slitted eye. I'm in a nest of the things. I jump out of the thicket only to land in another pile of the stupid seeds.

I jump backward and get clear.

Argh. Humph. Stupid things. Ouch. Stupid. Stupid. Stupid.
"Hiss."
Snarling doesn't get them off.
"Rrrr."
Growling doesn't work either, but it makes me feel better.
Stupid things have my whiskers all knotted up and my eyes half closed.
"Rrrrr."
There are some in my ear, and they tickle. They pull at my fur and tug my skin around my eye. Twitching makes it worse now. I can't even flick my tail.
Oh my gosh. It's folded and stuck to my side.
Argh.
I can't close my outer eyelid on the right side, but I can get the inner lid shut.
Boston will help. I hobble over to where she is reading at the picnic table. It's not easy. Those stupid things are stuck all over me and pull at my fur whenever I move.
Boston doesn't notice me. I wait a moment.
"Merow?"
Ow. That jerked my whiskers.
"Hey, Tiger," she says absently, not looking, so I repeat my cry a little louder.
"MEROW" *Ow.* That hurt more.
"What's up?" she asks lowering her book and turning to look at me.
I give her my poor pitiful look which isn't hard because I sure feel poor and pitiful with my lashes half glued to my cheek.

"Oh, my goodness. You poor thing." Shock, mixed with – amusement?

Better not be laughing.

"What happened?" She drops her book, and picks me up, sitting me in her lap.

I got into beggar lice. Whimper. Snivel.

This is so not cat-like. Not my normal sassy reply. At least I don't whine out loud. I'm not quite that pathetic. I'm a Maine Coon cat, I have some dignity, or I did before I turned green.

Ugh.

She pats my head.

Ow.

Some beggars stick to her hand. "Oh. Well. Let me see your poor head." She turns my head gently and examines my half-closed eye.

She reaches toward it and I automatically jerk away.

"It's okay, sweetie. Let me look." She reaches out again and this time I'm strong and control the jerk. She uses one hand to put some pressure on my eyelid and gently pulls off one of the seeds. I don't even feel the tug. She flicks it on the table and plucks a second.

Doesn't hurt me.

I lift my face to make it easier for her. Point my eyelashes at her. And my whiskers. Try to. Point my ears which still tickle.

Oh, hurry.

"Where were you? Where did you get these stick-ums?

Did you go across the street? You didn't go across the street, did you?"

Well. Earlier. Maybe I went across the street. But if I did, that squirrel made me do it and I'm not telling.

She gently plucks another one off. "You're not allowed across the street." She picks one off my whisker, tugging a little. Feels good to have it gone.

"These stickers grow on a plant with a really pretty purple flower. It wouldn't be so bad if the flower stuck to you. Maybe"

Stupid things. She'll show 'em.

"What in the world?" The deep voice makes me jerk and my whiskers pull.

Ow.

I hadn't heard Kevlar arrive. I try to glare at him.

"What have you got?" he asks, walking closer. "Is that Tiger? Why is he green? You both have stick-tights all over you."

Boston loosens her grip and I turn my poor, pitiful, pathetic face toward him. He's frowning, but his lip twitches and I hit him with a warning glare. The stick-tights don't make that easy.

He coughs the laugh away. "Let me help."

I edge away, but Boston pulls me back. "Start at his tail. Don't pull his fur. Make sure you have the base of the hair between your fingers before you tug the sticker. Kind of like when you work the snarls out of my hair."

Right.

He tugs some stick-ums.

"Ow. Maw."

"Ooops, sorry Tiger. I didn't realize those were stuck to fur from different spots. How did you do this? Your tail is actually pasted to your hip."

He starts again, gently, plucking the single stickers and soon I can stretch my tail out straight.

Ah, that feels so good. I try a small flick.

Boston unsnarls the whiskers on the left side of my face and stops to scrub lice off her hands into the pile on the table top and then plucks off the beggar stuck to my eyelid.

Sigh. Now, I can keep a wary eye on Kevlar. Don't know which makes me feel better.

They work together quietly, Boston untangling the right side where my nose itches. Soon, with just a little minor pulling, all my whiskers are free, and Boston moves to the longer thicker hair sensors above my right eye.

Kevlar grumbles, "What did he do? Roll in this stuff? They're all over him. Where did he even find a patch of weeds?" He works his way up my back and down my sides. His gentleness surprises me, but I flick my tail at him when he tugs a cluster of stickers, pulling fur.

That was dumb. Now my tail is stuck to my side again. It's his fault and I glare at him.

"Hold still," he orders not noticing my scowl, and grabs my tail firmly, but gently.

"Grrr." The growl is frustration and annoyance. If I were a dog, I'd whimper. This is so degrading. I can't believe I let Kevlar grab my tail, not once, but twice. The mental torment is as bad as the physical discomfort.

Beggar Lice

Boston has freed all the whiskers and lashes on my face and I can open and close both eyes now. I sigh with relief. She begins on the long sensor hairs on my front leg which are tangled and matted. "Tiger, you must have been rolling in the weeds to get this tangled."

Not rolling. Hunting. I'm a fierce Maine Coon cat.

She finishes with my paws and lifts me into the air. Shoves me onto Kevlar's lap.

"What the...," Kevlar says.

What???? No.

We're both taken by surprise, but it's too late for either of us to do anything. He grabs me by the shoulders and stands me upright on my back paws holding me tight.

We're face to face.

My front paws are on a line with his nose.

I could touch it.

Boston stands and brushes her lap. "I need to pull these stickers off my lap, so I can finish cleaning him. Otherwise they'll end up right back on him." She peels the stickers off her jeans and drops them in her pile on the table.

"But...," Kevlar says looking me in the eye. In fear?

My left paw twitches and taps his nose. He jerks his head back out of reach and that look in his eyes become stronger. It is fear. Or maybe just caution.

Cool.

We stare at each other for a very, very long time. Then he straightens his elbows, lifts me up on my tiptoes, and walks me backward four steps until my back paws are on his knees and my front claws can't reach his face. Then he lowers me down to stand comfortably on all four legs. But he keeps that grip on my shoulders with my front legs grasped tight between his thumbs and forefingers.

Chicken. I didn't even have my claws out when I tapped him.

His chin and nose are safely out of reach.

We stare at each other and then I look around for Boston. She's rubbing beggar-lice off her jeans. What? Is she introducing herself to each one?

Save me.

She finally grabs me back and lays me on her lap, belly up, my back wedged between her thighs, my head against her stomach, my feet sticking in the air. "Now I can work on his stomach. You want to start on his back paws?" she asks Kevlar.

No. Not happening. I struggle to turn over.

Kick at his hand when he reaches for my leg. My claws out this time.

"Stop that," Boston says.

Kevlar reaches for my leg again and I pull it away.

Really. A cat's back legs are private.

Kevlar takes a step back. "Ah. I, ah, I think I'll leave the cat to you," he says, nervously.

Good.

We both look at him. He takes another step back.

Smart man. He might get hurt if he grabs my foot again.

"I think, yes, I think I need to find out where he was. These weeds will take over the area if I don't get them mown." He backs off and doesn't try to touch me again.

Maybe, he's more scared then smart. Either way he has come up with a good excuse to leave. Work.

Boston motions with her head. "He came from around the building." She peels some lice off my belly.

My right paw is twitchy, and I push it up to her. She missed a beggar. She doesn't notice, so I wave my paw in front of her face. "How can I see to pull these things off if you block my view?" she asks and grabs my paw to push it out of the way.

"Oh, I missed this, and it has your paw feelers, longer whiskers? Receptors? Sensors? whatever they are called, snarled, and glued together. I'll have to look up the right word. Poor Tiger

That's right.

She holds the whisker base firmly against my paw and tugs the stickum off.

Ahhh. That's better.

I nestle between her legs, almost relaxed and she finishes with my belly and starts on my back legs, I keep an eye on her and tentatively test movement.

Whiskers all work fine. Eyes, open and close. Ears? All clear. Same with my mouth. Okay. Ready to get back to that bird. I start to lift myself and she says, "One more," and plucks it off. "There. All done."

Before I can move she puts a kiss on my head and sets me on the ground.

Well. Whatever. I shake myself. But I need a long grooming session to put my coat in order which will have to wait until I get my bird.

Kevlar rounds the corner and walks stiffly toward us holding something. His legs are green. Not the green of Park Service jeans. The green of stick-ums. Guess he found them.

"Where have you been?" Boston asks with a laugh in her voice. "You look like a green abombd, abonidable, wait. I'll get the word." She holds up a hand as he walks over. "Abominable snowman." She laughs out loud. "You look like Tiger did before we de-liced him."

I laugh too. His legs, to above his knees, are covered in beggar lice. As are his arms up to his elbows. His whole front is green. I see a couple on his eyebrow. And he's holding a ball of beggar-lice and leaves in his hands close to his chest.

"What do you have?" Boston asks and stands for a closer look.

He opens some fingers and shows her my bird.

I go on alert. Not beggar lice.

My bird.

He has my bird.

"I think your cat chased this fella into a patch of stick-tights.

Me? Not me. I don't chase birds. I'm a conservator.

My bird has stick-tight beggar-lice matted through his feathers, gluing and tangling the leafy vine all around him, pinning his wings.

"Poor little fella," Boston says.

Poor little fella? It's all his fault. He lured me into those weeds. He's the reason I got so sticky.

Beggar Lice

"It's a sparrow hawk, American kestrel," she says in wonder. "I've never been this close to one."

I have. Almost a lot closer too.

The sparrow hawks sit way up high on the overhead power lines. They sometimes holler, 'Kill e, Kill y, Kill e'. They're supposed to catch sparrows, but we don't have many sparrows here. Because we have sparrow hawks? I've seen them eat grasshoppers and lizards. Yuk. Grasshoppers taste like stringy twigs and lizards make me sick. Not that I've eaten any.

This kestrel is the smallest and most common of the falcons, about the size of a blue jay. His head and wing patches are slate blue or Payne's Grey. Boston says that's the proper name of the color. Bold black slashes, two of them, run from his eye to under his chin and he has a rusty brown back and wings. The female is a dull, plain brown. Birds are strange the way the females are different colors from the males

I glare at Kevlar. *He's mine.* I would have caught him, but the beggar lice got me. *Mine.*

But Kevlar sits, holding the bird away from me and toward Boston. "I'll hold his head and talons while you work on him. He bit me good a couple of times and clawed me with his talons, too." He moves his arm and shows the blood dripping through his fingers.

Wow. He let my bird bite him?

"Let me see." Boston reaches for his bloody hand.

"It will keep. Let's get this bird cleaned up first."

I sit in front of Kevlar's knee and ask politely, "Merow?"

Then reach up for my bird, but he brushes me gently away with the back of his hand.

"No Tiger. This is wildlife. Mine," he says. That's the word he uses when he doesn't want me to touch his stuff. He's serious when he says it.

But the bird is mine. I sit on my haunches and keep a close watch. Maybe I'll get the kestrel when they're done.

He tells Boston, "Start with the stick-tights first. The vine is tangled all through his feathers, tacked down by the stick-tights. It's wrapped tight around him."

Boston examines the green bird closely.

"Right. Good thinking. Stick-tights first, then the vine. He'll try to fly as soon as his wings are free, and we want him stickum free then. Where did you find him?" she asks, holding the feathers gently while plucking off the beggar seeds.

"In some, ah, weeds, under your buddy Dell's stairs. He was backed into a corner hidden in the shadow. Cowering like you might expect if a cat had chased it."

He frowns at me.

Not me. I wasn't chasing it. More like watching. Closely.

"What else," Boston asks. "There's something you're not saying."

He hesitates a moment. Has me curious now too. "The weeds he was in? A patch of home grown pot."

Pot? I didn't see any pots. Besides you don't grow pots, you buy them. People buy them.

"No way. Dell's growing pot? Under his stairs?" She giggles. Thinks a moment. Laughs out loud, still pulling stick-ums.

"Sure, he's growing pot. But seriously? Right out there in the open? That's pretty bold. Must have been high when he planted them there. Hah. Growing drugs under the stairs."

Do they mean those fowl smelling weeds? Not pots, but weeds?

Boston is still laughing. "Why am I not surprised? And he's not my buddy. Just a guy I work with. I can't believe he thinks no one will find his garden. How did he think he could get away with it? I mean, when he sobered up."

"Didn't think, I'd guess. You're probably right. He was high when he planted them."

Boston nodded. "Sure. And he wouldn't expect anyone to go under his stairs. He'd think his patch would be safe there. Besides, the stuff is almost legal in Florida."

"Almost. And that's state law not federal. Marijuana is still against federal law and we're federal. It isn't legal in the park under federal law. Del could be in big trouble."

"What are you going to do?" she asks.

"Think about it."

She nods, pulling one last stick-tight off my bird. "There, I have all the beggar-lice off this guy, let me have your Buck knife and I'll cut the vine."

"It's in my right pocket."

She fiddles around for the knife and I reach for my bird again. Boston pats me on the head. "No. Tiger. You can't have him. He's protected."

Sheesh.

"I'll get you some tuna when we go in."

Okay, maybe.

She slips Kevlar's knife under the vine loops and the leaves fall off except for one strand which she gently unwraps.

Kevlar opens his hands and the bird freezes a moment, shakes his feathers, spreads his wings and, like lightening, he shoots into the air and away.

Gone.

He lands on the powerline and shakes his feathers again. They're all puffed up and he looks really chubby.

Sparrow Hawk

"Beautiful," Boston says.

They watch my bird until he takes off and flies into the trees and disappears and then Boston asks Kevlar again, "What are you going to do? You can't turn Dell into Catfish. Catfish doesn't like him and will arrest him, and he'll lose his job and go to jail."

I don't like Catfish. He's a mean person. Doesn't like cats.

Kevlar nods his head. "Yeah, that's what I figure, too. Catfish won't cut him any slack. But I can't take the chance one of my men will find the plants when mowing. I think I'm going to send out a notice to all residents that I'll be sending a work crew in the at end of the week to complete our bi-annual cleanup around the buildings. Which is true. I have to get those weeds, um, the stick-tight weeds, out of there. I'll request everyone move their personal things out of the area, so we can manicure around the houses and trailers and under the stairs and decks."

She gives him a big smile and a hug. "You are so smart," she says, then leans back and looks down at herself. "Uh-oh. We just shared your stick-tights. Let's clean these off and go inside and I'll make some tuna sandwiches for lunch.

Lunch? My favorite meal. Especially tuna.

BACON WRAPPED FRIED CHICKEN NUGGETS

Jackson's having a party. Boston and Kevlar are sharing the hosting because our two apartments are across the screened in breezeway from each other. With both front doors open, people can wander back and forth. Parties are good. There's lots of food. This party is for Sluggo. Killer, Jackson calls him. Killer is a hero because he rescued me. It should have been my party, after all, he couldn't have done it without me. And, besides, I saved him before he saved me. I should get a party.

Boston made some good stuff, and after I secure my snack, I walk over to explore Sluggo's house and see what Jackson made. I've never been in there. The place smells slightly of dog. Sluggo to be exact. I check out some of his toys, but he doesn't have any catnip. Sniff his food dish. Ugh. His water dish is empty. He doesn't care because he is working the room, begging. And eating snacks. A dog bone shaped cookie. Yuk. Why not a dog bone shaped hamburger? That would make more sense. But he's such a dog, he doesn't care.

Watching Sluggo eat reminds me I'm still hungry, even though I'm full, so I go back to my own snack. I sit looking at it, wishing I could eat more when Sluggo walks in. I like Sluggo, but I don't want him eating from my food dishes or using my litter box, so I stalk over, arch my back and growl and he heads back to his own house.

Since I can't fit in any more food, I decide to nap and don't wake up until the party is over and Boston and Kevlar are cleaning up.

"Hey, the party worked out pretty good, didn't it," Boston says, picking up some empty beer cans. "Every time I saw Killer someone was giving him some kind of food. Did you see the dog tray they gave him?"

"Missed that. A whole tray?"

"Yeah." She smiles. "It had raw hamburg balls, ham and cheese chunks, and beef jerky. A doggy buffet."

What? I didn't see that.

"I liked the tag for his collar - hero cat saver. Not very good English, but we all know what it means. I can't believe we had a party because a dog rescued a cat." Kevlar shakes his head.

"The cat was Tiger," Boston says. "Killer deserves to be honored." She tosses the empties in a garbage can and picks up some used paper plates. "Did you sample the bacon wrapped fried chicken nuggets?" she asks. "By the time I got a chance to try them, I couldn't even find the platter. Did you try one? How were they?"

Oops.

"Now that you mention it," Kevlar says, "I don't remember seeing them and I was kind of hoping to snag a couple. Two of my favorite food groups together and fried. I don't know how you came up with the idea, but it works for me. They must have been eaten right away. Did anyone mention them?"

Uh-oh. Bacon wrapped fried chicken nuggets are my all-time favorite. They were good. Kevlar doesn't know what he missed. Most of the nuggets are in my tummy. I haven't been able to eat them all and I look longingly at the three remaining nuggets. Cats don't beg like dogs, they forage for themselves and I foraged the platter of fried chicken and bacon nuggets, I liberated them, rescued the platter. I slid it to the edge of the table, onto the chair, and from there to the floor where it tumbled over. Didn't hurt the nuggets.

I glance down at the three remaining morsels. Hope Boston isn't going to look for them. But I better hide them. I give the empty plate a nudge and get it almost under the chair and tap a loose morsel beside it.

I try to hide the second nugget under my back foot.

Kevlar says, "I looked for it and then got distracted by the clams casino which Bob brought. Did you try those. Really good."

"Yeah, I think I ate three." She changes the subject. "Did you see Killer? Everyone was sneaking him food. That was cute. I'm happy Tiger doesn't do that. Beg, I mean. He's a good cat."

"Yeah, Killer looked happy begging treats. He sure snarfed them down. You know, I don't remember even seeing Tiger tonight," Kevlar says as they both walk toward the kitchen and the piles of leftovers.

Uh-oh. Boston's moving in my direction and I don't have time to put my front paw in front of the nugget under my back foot. No time to hide this last chicken nugget. I quickly stuff it in my mouth. The whole thing.

Oops. It doesn't fit. My mouth is so full I can't gulp it or swallow. Parts are hanging down over my chin.

Hide, I need to hide.

I won't fit under the chair and don't have time to edge that way and hide behind it.

"Tiger," Boston calls looking around. "Where are you?" she turns and looks straight at me.

Caught.

I lift only my eyes. Maybe she won't notice the nugget.

"Tiger," she says in outrage. With, hopefully, a little touch of humor? Pride? Maybe. I'll play on that. Sometimes she thinks I'm so cute she forgets to scold me.

I try a smile.

Drool and chicken juice dribble out the corners of my mouth and down my neck.

Forgot my mouth is stuffed.

Her lips work, but no sound comes out. Kevlar cuts off a snort. He's standing behind her and his cheeks are kind of sucked in and his lips are twitching. He tries to hide it with his fist.

He better not be laughing.

Bacon Wrapped Fried Chicken Nuggets

Tiger Caught with Nuggets

I don't take my eyes off Boston.

He is laughing. I hear it. He's laughing at me. He'll pay for that.

"Tiger." Boston orders. "Put that down."

Ordinarily I wouldn't obey, but I can't swallow the

thing and the drool is embarrassing and Kevlar is laughing at me.

I lean forward and gently drop it on the floor. Close to the front of my paws where I can snatch it back. A small drool pool forms around it.

I lift my eyes back to Boston.

"What did you do?" She's standing with her fists on her hips, looking at me sternly. Trying to. Her lips are curved up and one hand keeps sneaking across her mouth. To stop the laugh.

Kevlar turns away. His shoulders are shaking.

I'll deal with him.

I try my innocent look.

"Don't you try that innocent look on me. I see that platter half under the chair."

I look down. She's right, I don't have it hidden.

"And what are those nuggets doing on the floor?"

Well, it should be obvious. I haven't been able to eat them. Yet. I look at them sadly.

"Four, five of them," she says, counting.

Five?

That many? I missed five? Now I am really sad.

"You are a bad, bad cat. Go to your room."

Hunh? She's sending me to the bedroom?

But Kevlar stops her. "You might not want to do that, honey. He's pretty greasy right now."

She looks me up and down and sucks in her cheeks.

Laughing. I know she's laughing.

Bacon Wrapped Fried Chicken Nuggets

"Right." She jerks her head toward the deck door. "Out there. Go."

I give her my best unhappy, adorable, puppy-dog imitation.

She ignores it and grabs a napkin off the table and wipes it down my neck and chest. I try to back up, but her other sneaky hand has the back of my neck and she holds me tight. She wipes again. When I struggle, she tosses the napkin aside, picks me up, carries me to the door, and sets me out on the deck. She quickly ducks back inside, slamming the door behind her.

Well. The deck's not bad, but the nuggets are inside. Five of them. The louvered glass windows are still wide open from the party.

"I'll be back with your litter box," she says.

Oh-oh. Does she plan on leaving me out here all night? In the dark? Out in the wilderness? Alone? She can't be. That would be cat abuse.

I know I'm a cat and dark and night are okay, but it's the principle of the thing. You don't throw your favorite cat out in the dark, in the wilderness, in the middle of the night, all alone. And sure, it's not really outside, it's the deck, the Florida room. But jeeze. What about my water dish? And my toys? And my blankee. Okay I don't have a blankee, but I could have one if I wanted to.

I watch through the glass louvers as she falls into Kevlar's arms convulsing in laughter.

Both of them. Laughing.

At me.

"I can't believe he ate all those nuggets. He's only one cat," she says through giggles

"Probably the reason some are left, he couldn't fit any more inside his sagging tummy."

Sagging tummy? Oh, he is so in trouble.

Kevlar chuckles. "Did you see that innocent look on his face? With the evidence hanging out of his mouth and dribbling down his front?"

Laughing. Both of them. Still. You'd think they'd get tired of that.

Traitors.

She wipes her eyes. "I'll never forget that innocent look. Did he think I wouldn't notice that huge piece of chicken hanging out of his mouth?" She shakes her head. "Silly cat." She says that almost with admiration and shrugs her shoulders. "Guess I better go clean up that mess. He tracked grease all over the floor and that slobber puddle is disgusting."

She chuckles again, not too mad. Getting over it. "I'm going to remember that look when I'm old and gray."

I watch her wipe the floor with paper towels and then wash it with a rag.

I would have licked that clean. I was going to finish the nuggets first, and then lick the floor clean.

She picks up the platter and puts the nuggets on it.

My nuggets. Is she going to bring them out here? I sit up.

"What are you going to do with those?" Kevlar asks my question.

Yeah, what?

"Hate to throw them out." she says. "I was thinking I could give them to him."

Yes, perfect.

"That would be rewarding bad behavior."

No, it would be frugal.

"Yeah. But I hate to heave them. They were a lot of work."

"Wash them off. Give him the chicken one day, the bacon the next. He won't make the connection."

Won't make the connection? I won't make the connection? That man is in deep trouble. I'm thinking his toothbrush definitely is going in my litter box.

Wait. He just told her to give me the snacks. He is a good, kind, thoughtful man. His toothbrush is safe. For now.

"I was really looking forward to those," he adds. "Maybe you can make them again soon. For you and me?"

"I don't know. Like I said, they were a lot of work." She pauses. "I did want a couple for myself, though." She snorts again. "That face. I will never forget that face. The chicken and bacon hanging out of his mouth. Slobber leaking out and dribbling down his neck." She giggles. "Well, how can I be mad at him when he's so entertaining?"

They walk into the kitchen where I can't see them, but I hear the refrigerator door open. I hope she's saving my nuggets.

They can't see me, so I try to squeeze through the

louvers. I can get my head through. And a paw. That's it. No way can I get my shoulders through, the opening is way too small for a Maine Coon cat. I stand on my back toes to see if I can maybe climb up higher. Nope.

They come back into the room.

"Meow?"

Boston looks straight at me. "No, you are a bad cat. A very bad cat. Stay out there." But her mouth keeps trying to curve up around the scolding. That's a good sign.

She shrugs and says to Kevlar. "He usually likes it out there. But because he's being punished, I guess he thinks it a jail."

It is a jail. I will not go quietly into this night. **"MEROWW".**

"You holler all you want, you're spending the night out there," Boston says in her stern voice.

Mean. "Meow?"

Kevlar touches her arm. "Are you sure you want to encourage him? It could get noisy. Maybe if he can't see us, he'll settle down. Let's go out front out of sight."

They Go Out The Front Door. *Rrghhh.*

Well, really. They left. Just like that. They walk away and leave me locked up out here in the dark. Alone. *Arghh.* I flick my tail. Not fair. I flick it again.

Five? I missed five? Darn.

I continue voicing my complaints, but tire of it quickly. It's boring and I may be getting hoarse.

I stop hollering and look around. There's nothing to tear up, and Boston might get angry if I did something really bad. Right now, she's sort of angry, but more impressed with my cleverness. She was laughing. That laugh which has a speck of pride. Sure it's mixed with a little anger, but that will pass.

I look for something to do until they come back. She hasn't brought my litter pan, so I can't scratch litter over the floor.

Nothing inside the room. I check the backyard, no night critters hunting. There's a flashing light out on the bay. Irregular flashing. But, it's just a boat. Phooey.

A rattling up near the ceiling.

Aha. A cricket near the top of the screen. Crickets are fun. I test the screen. I'm sure it will hold me. Boston has said I can't tear it, but she's never said I can't climb it. I climb slowly up and I'm almost to the cricket when Kevlar hollers through the window, "What are you doing?"

I jerk. I hadn't heard them come back.

Snap.

What?

I look at the sound and see a screen thread is split and I watch in horror as another splits around my claw.

Snip. Snap. Snap. Multiple threads snap and a v forms at my claw.

Ack! Snap.

All my right paw claws are tearing the screen. This is so not like climbing the coconut palm.

Zing.

Oops. Now my left front paw claws tear through the screen.

Zing. Snap. Zing.

I try to slow myself with my back feet and those claws cut through the threads like butter and I'm tearing the screen with all four feet as I begin a slow slide down.

Stupid screen.

Zing. Pop. Pop. Zap. Zing. Zing. Like a little machine gun. Rat a tat tat.

"Tiger get off that screen," Boston yells.

I would if I could, but I can't let go, I don't have enough leverage to jump off and I can't stop the downward motion.

I am in deep trouble.

Stop. Stop. Stupid screen.

Kevlar whips open the door and grabs me before I can slide more than a couple of feet.

"What was he doing up there? He never climbs the screen," Boston says looking up. "Oh, a cricket. It must have attracted him."

Kevlar shakes his head, holding me by the shoulders out at arm's length. "Are you making an excuse for him?"

"No. Just wanted to understand why he was climbing the screen." She touches the gouges my claws made. "Going to be tough to replace. Maintenance is going to be angry."

"I am maintenance," Kevlar says, "and I am already angry. But I'll fix the screen. There's no reason for us to mention the cat's bad behavior. Or we can say you tore it, if you prefer. Not the very bad, very overweight cat."

Bacon Wrapped Fried Chicken Nuggets

Tiger Climbing Screen

I am not overweight. I'm thinking toothbrush in the litter box again.

"I'll fix it in the morning, and we won't tell anyone."

She smiles sweetly. "My hero." Then she turns to me

and says, "My very bad cat. Twice in one night. Twice that we know about."

She doesn't know yet. But that other thing wasn't really my fault.

She doesn't try to touch me but leans over and looks me in the eye. "Bad, bad cat."

I think I still see a smile hidden and blink my eyes.

"What's that flashing light?" Kevlar asks.

They both stare at it and Kevlar forgets he's angry and pulls me close to his chest.

I freeze.

He stares at the flashing light. "It's Morse Code, well sort of. Maybe. Might be an SOS. If it's Morse, it would be three short, three long, three short. This is two long, two short, and two long. Nothing else, just two, two, two, over and over. Someone must be broken down. I'll call Bob, he's on duty tonight."

Kevlar looks at me suddenly realizing he's holding me and hands me to Boston and heads inside. We follow. I guess I'm furloughed. Or is that paroled? Pardoned? Sprung? Anyhow, I'm not going to mention I'm released.

After he makes the call, they finish the cleanup. I check under the table and chair in case Boston missed a nugget. Bummer. Then sit politely in front of my food dish looking at her hopefully.

"No. Tiger. No food. You had your dinner before the party and don't remind me that you are stuffed with my chicken nuggets."

Well darn.

Bacon Wrapped Fried Chicken Nuggets

There is some radio chatter and we go to the deck to watch the Ranger boat speed out on its rescue mission which I find very boring. I fetch my mouse and play with him.

"Did you talk to Shorty tonight at the party?" Kevlar asks.

"Didn't get a chance. Why?"

"He's adopting those two dogs."

"What? But they're wild. That black one tried to kill Tiger and he hurt Killer."

Yes. He tried to kill me.

"He says they're not bad, just not trained. Those two jerks picked them up at the pound last week and let them run wild."

Boston has a frown on her face. "You think they're teachable?"

"Shorty trains dogs, he says these two will make good service dogs. He wanted to make sure it was all right with me. And Jackson. Since they hurt Killer and tried to murder my cat."

What? I'm not your cat.

Boston laughed at him. "So now you have cat. That's cute. How do you feel about that?"

He and I stare at each other. I can feel a little growl in my throat. *Be careful here boy*, I warn him silently.

"I guess if I had to have a cat, Tiger would be the one I'd want."

Okay.

More radio chatter and a call for the ambulance to

meet them at the ramp and the rangers tow the other boat back.

We're resting on the hateful deck, when Bob knocks on our door and walks in. "Hello. Wanted to thank you and let you know how it turned out."

"They run aground?" Kevlar asks.

"Yeah. Sort of. But they weren't fishing."

"Birding?" Boston asks with a frown. "At night?"

Bob shakes his head with a funny smile. "Get this." He pauses dramatically. "They were gigging for frogs. Three guys out there gigging for frogs."

"Gigging for frogs in the bay? In the salt water?" Boston asks puzzled. "There aren't any frogs out there."

Bob raises his hand. "I swear. Honest. Gigging for frogs. I have never met three so dimwitted, brainless, stupid idiots. Not drunk, just jerks. I asked why they're gigging in the bay and one goon pipes up 'because it's illegal to gig in the ponds'. Goon two says he told them it's illegal in the bay too. Goon three tells them both to shut up because no one can prove they were gigging because they don't have any frogs. Goon two says it's goon three's fault they ran aground because he wouldn't let them use running lights. Goon three said he didn't want anyone to see the lights."

Bob snorts. "Like no one can see the spotlight they use to find the frogs?" He shakes his head. "They finally gave up and headed back to the marina. Straight back. They didn't want to go all the way around and didn't follow the channel. Ran aground and burned up the engine trying to get off the mud flat. Then goon one tried to use the push-pole. Called it a stick. He stuck it in the mud and tried to pull the boat to it. Lost his balance, tumbled and fell over the gunnels and broke his arm. Goon two got so excited he threw down his gig and speared goon three's foot." He shook his head. "Who lets these people out on the water? And they were sober."

I hop up into Boston's lap and she absent mindedly scratches my ears.

Forgiven.

Bob finishes his story. "If you hadn't reported the flashes, we wouldn't have found them until daylight. It would have been a very uncomfortable night for them on the water, but not deadly." He grabbed the cold beer Kevlar offered. "They kept the squabbling up all the time and gave me a headache. Two seasonals are running them into the hospital."

He took a long drink of beer. "How did you spot them?"

Kevlar points to me. "Tiger pointed them. We'd locked him out on the back deck."

"He always stay on the deck at night?"

"No. We were punishing him."

Bob looks at me with a quizzical smile. "Oh. What did he do?"

Boston pokes me gently. "He ate the bacon wrapped fried chicken nuggets."

"Bacon wrapped chicken nuggets? Fried? I didn't see any of those. Got any left?"

Kevlar smiles, shakes his head because the cat took the whole platter a...

"If there's five left, I could eat one or ..." says hopefully.

Not my nuggets. No way. Those are mine. And I go... one now. Maybe two. I look hopefully.

"They were on the floor and, knowing Tiger, he probably licked them all." Kevlar says that with a bit of pride.

I did. Or would have if I'd had time. I was too busy eating to be lapping.

Bob busts out laughing, and they join him and embroider the tale of how they caught me. Exaggerating the drool and dribble.

I don't like that story.

Kevlar says, "We had this party for Killer tonight. We need another party. One for Tiger. After all, Tiger saved Killer from the snake, and Jeffy from the scorpion, and that kestrel from the evil stick-tights, and he did help rescue those idiots tonight. And Boston can make more bacon wrapped fried chicken nuggets."

Yay. Yay.

Boston considers it.

What? I nudge her. *Of course, I should have a party.*

"It's a good idea. We need an excuse for a party. Let's do it next weekend. And this time I'll make sure the chicken nuggets are out of his reach. Or maybe I'll make them with a spinach, kale center," she adds.

Ugh.

Bob snorts and asks, "Why would you do that? Ruin a perfect snack with green stuff?"

"Spinach and kale are good for you," she says righteously.

I've heard her say spinach makes her fingernails strong. I've also heard her say it tastes like green construction paper. It doesn't. Not that I've eaten either. Well, maybe once, each, by mistake. The paper is sweeter than the spinach.

"Besides," she nods toward me. "It will slow him down."

"You make them, I'll guard them. No green stuff," Bob offers. "Maybe make some for Tiger."

Oh, what a good idea. I like Ranger Bob.

"I don't know." Kevlar shakes his head.

What. His toothbrush is going in the litter box for sure. Don't listen to him Boston.

"I don't think he'd enjoy them as much if you just give them to him," Kevlar says.

Razor too I think.

He continues. "Maybe put some on a paper plate and leave the plate where he can reach it when no one is looking."

I love him better than Ranger Bob. Listen to him Boston. My own platter.

Yes. More bacon wrapped chicken nuggets. Who cares if they have green centers. I'm a Maine Coon cat. I'll eat the outside. Leave the green innards for Sluggo. He's a dog; he'll eat anything.

Don't miss Tiger's Adventures in the Everglades, Volume Three

jay gee heath also writes romantic mystery and mystery with romance
Visit her web page at http://www.jaygeeheath.com/

Contact her at jaygeeheath@gmail.com

www.ingramcontent.com/pod-product-compliance
Lightning Source LLC
Chambersburg PA
CBHW051601010526
44118CB00023B/2781